Seymour Simon

SEE MORE READERS

P9-CEI-280

DANGER!
EARTHQUAKES

SeaStar Books · San Francisco

This book is dedicated to my granddaughter Chloe.

Special thanks to reading consultant Dr. Linda B. Gambrell, Director of the School of Education at Clemson University, past president of the National Reading Conference, and past board member of the International Reading Association.

Permission to use the following photographs is gratefully acknowledged:
front cover: © David Weintraub, Photo Researchers, Inc.; title page, page 32: Mehmet Celebi, U.S. Geological Survey; pages 2–3: M. Hopper, U.S. Geological Survey; pages 4–5, 26-27: D. Perkins, U.S. Geological Survey; pages 6–9, 22–23: National Geophysical Data Center; pages 10–11: J. Dewey, U.S. Geological Survey; pages 14–15: University of Colorado; pages 16–17: © Van Bucher, Photo Researchers, Inc.; pages 18–19, 30–31: Earthquake Engineering Research Institute; pages 20–21: U.S. Geological Survey, Menlo Park, CA; pages 24–25: Reinsurance Company, Munich, Germany.

SeaStar is an imprint of Chronicle Books LLC.

Library of Congress Cataloging-in-Publication Data is available.

ISBN 1-58717-140-6

Distributed in Canada by Raincoast Books
9050 Shaughnessy Street, Vancouver, British Columbia V6P 6E5

10 9 8 7 6 5 4 3

Chronicle Books LLC
85 Second Street, San Francisco, California 94105

www.chroniclekids.com

The ground beneath your feet
may seem solid.
But earthquakes make
the ground shake and roll.

Most earthquakes last
a minute or less.
Yet they cause more damage
than any other natural disaster.
Earthquakes can knock down
buildings and wreck highways.
They can destroy whole cities
and towns.

Each year, there are
about a million earthquakes
around the world.
But only about 100 of these
cause much damage.
Fewer than 20 result in deaths.

The worst earthquakes can kill
thousands of people.
In Italy, 85,000 people died when
a dangerous quake hit in 1908.

Scientists use the Richter scale
to measure an earthquake's
power.
You may not even notice
a magnitude 2 quake.

You would feel the ground shake
in a magnitude 3 quake.
A magnitude 7 or higher
can destroy a city.
The largest recorded earthquake
was an 8.5 in Chile in 1960.

The Mercalli scale tells us
how much damage
an earthquake caused.
You would not feel a Level 1 quake.
Windows break at Level 5.
Level 12 is the worst.
Everything is totally destroyed.

The earthquake that shook
San Francisco in October 1989
measured 7.1 on the Richter scale.
On the Mercalli scale,
it measured from 6 to 11
in different parts of the city.

Most of the world's earthquakes
happen in a zone called the
Pacific Ring of Fire.

Most earthquakes begin
in the earth's crust.
The crust is a layer of rocks
that covers the earth.
It is 5 to 30 miles deep.
Cracks in the rocks run
through the crust.

These are called fault zones.
The rocks on one side
of a crack push against
the rocks on the other side.
The rocks may stay in place for
years, but then they suddenly
slide past each other.

What makes the rocks move?
The answer lies below the crust,
in the mantle.
The mantle is a 2,000-mile-thick
layer of melted rock.
Over millions of years,
movements in the mantle have
cracked the crust into huge
floating pieces called plates.

These plates grind
past each other
at about two inches per year.
That's about as fast as
your fingernails grow.
The layers of rock in this photo
folded because of
movements in the mantle.

The San Andreas fault lies between the North American and the Pacific plates. It runs for 700 miles through Southern California to just north of San Francisco.

Each year, California has about 35,000 earthquakes. Most are too small to be felt. Less than 100 measure 4 or more on the Richter scale.

Alaska has more earthquakes
than any other state.
Alaska has a magnitude 7 quake
almost every year.
Earthquakes also occur
in the central United States.
In 1811, an 8+ quake shook
the Mississippi valley.
It caused church bells to ring in
Boston, nearly 1,000 miles away.

The most violent earthquake
ever recorded in the United
States took place in Anchorage,
Alaska, in March 1964.
The quake measured 8.4
on the Richter scale
and 10 on the Mercalli scale.
Cracks in the earth up to 30 feet
wide opened like giant jaws.
Nearby ports were completely
destroyed by huge sea waves.
More than 100 people died.

In September 1985,
an 8.1 earthquake
struck Mexico City.
The quake was more powerful
than 1,000 atomic bombs.
Nearly 10,000 people were killed.

Hundreds of buildings
were destroyed.
Since then, stronger buildings
have been erected.
These new buildings
are much safer.

Some buildings remain standing
during a strong earthquake,
while others nearby collapse.
Building on steep hillsides
or on loose soil is dangerous.
It's safer to build a house
on flat land and solid rock.
The safest buildings
can bend back and forth
without breaking.

Scientists use machines
that can measure and record
earthquake activity.
They can also tell us where
earthquakes are likely to strike.

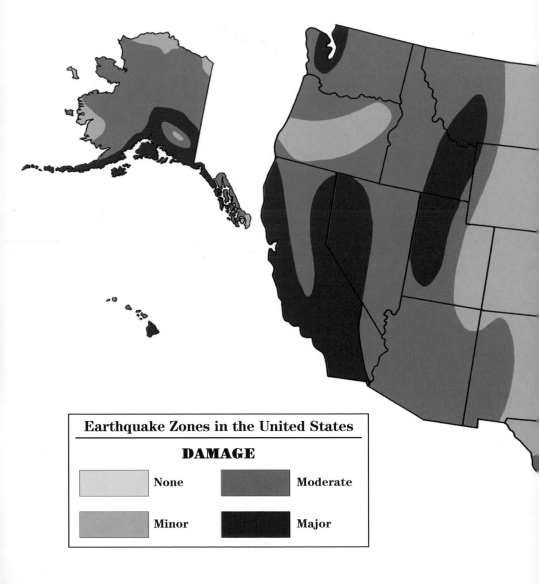

Earthquake Zones in the United States

DAMAGE

None

Minor

Moderate

Major

But they cannot yet tell us exactly when, where, or how big an earthquake will be.

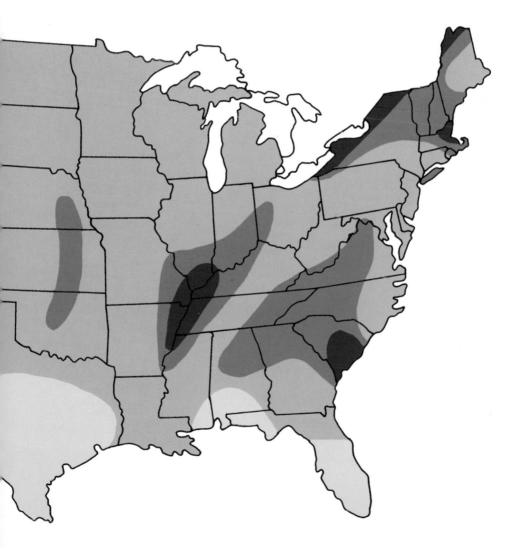

Here is what to do
if you are in an earthquake.
If you are indoors, stay there.
Take cover under a sturdy table,
desk, or bed.
Stay away from windows,
mirrors, and high cabinets.
If you are outdoors,
move away from power lines
and tall buildings.

No one can prevent earthquakes. But in the future we will be able to reduce the damage they cause.